A Snowy Day

By Jenna Lee Gleisner

SPARKS

Picture Glossary

cold   10

deep   6

2

The snow is falling.

falling

The snow is deep.

deep

The snow is white.

white

The snow is cold.

cold

The snow is pretty.

pretty

The snow is fun.

fun

The snow is _____.

falling

deep

white

cold

pretty

fun